TWISTED DARK

Volume 1

Jeremy!

By

Neil Gibson

Help spread the word!

Published by T Publications.

Special thanks to Luke Apps for his work behind the scenes.

To Louisa, for everything.

This is a book by Neil Gibson, not Mel Gibson. In case there is any confusion, there is a guide below:

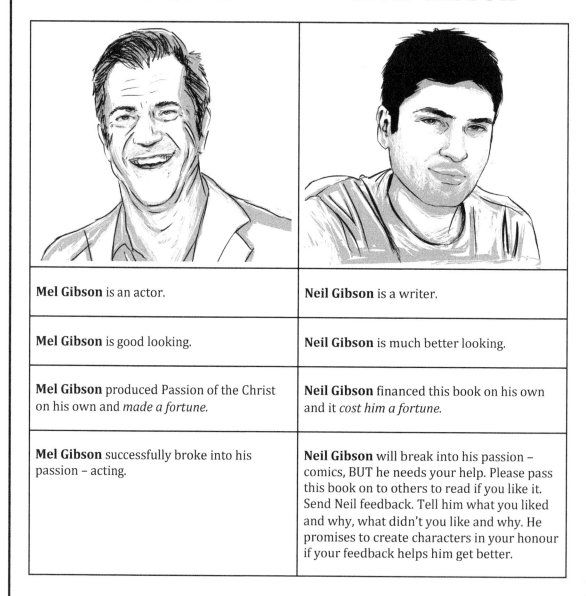

Mel Gibson	Neil Gibson
Mel Gibson is an actor.	**Neil Gibson** is a writer.
Mel Gibson is good looking.	**Neil Gibson** is much better looking.
Mel Gibson produced Passion of the Christ on his own and *made a fortune.*	**Neil Gibson** financed this book on his own and it *cost him a fortune.*
Mel Gibson successfully broke into his passion – acting.	**Neil Gibson** will break into his passion – comics, BUT he needs your help. Please pass this book on to others to read if you like it. Send Neil feedback. Tell him what you liked and why, what didn't you like and why. He promises to create characters in your honour if your feedback helps him get better.

You can find more comics for free at www.neilgibsoncomics.com, including previews of new titles.

Contents

Suicide...

Online chat rooms allow complete anonymity
Complete anonymity
You can tell strangers things that you wouldn't ever
want to reveal to your friends or family
You can release years of guilt and have the cathartic
feeling of confessing

Or...

You can just talk about how you really feel...

Writer/Creator
Neil Gibson

Illustrator
Atula Siriwardane

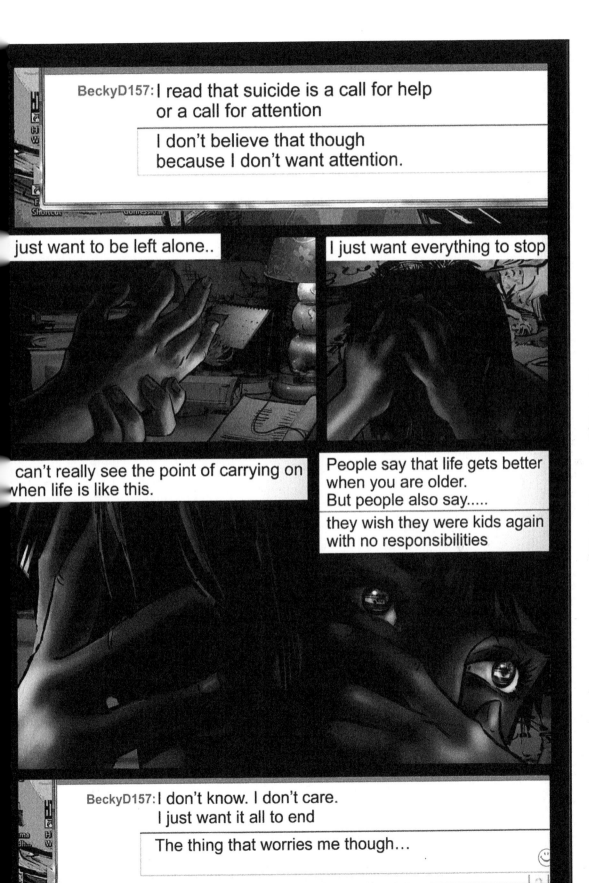

....is that I am only 10.

Routine...

Writer/Creator
Neil Gibson

Illustrator
Caspar Wijngaard

ASBJORN AND HIS SON HAD A ROUTINE...

KOLL!, YOU HARDLY TOUCHED YOUR FOOD!

SORRY DAD, NOT HUNGRY!

WHEN HE DIDN'T HAVE SCHOOL, KOLL WOULD TAKE THE DOG AND GO HUNTING,

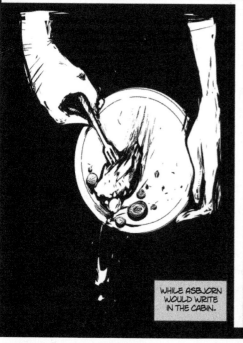

DON'T DAWDLE OR THE DAY WILL BE GONE!

WHILE ASBJORN WOULD WRITE IN THE CABIN.

IT WAS A SIMPLE PEACEFUL LIFE AND THEY LIKED IT.

THEY LIVED IN A VERY ISOLATED PART OF NORWAY ON THE ISLAND OF VÆRØY.

THE CLOSEST NEIGHBOURS WERE IN THE LITTLE FISHING VILLAGE OF MÅSTAD.

HE KNEW THAT THIS PLACE WAS TOO SMALL. IT WOULDN'T HOLD HIS SON FOREVER.

NO ONE BOTHERED THEM AND THAT SUITED ASBJORN JUST FINE.

KOLL WOULD GROW UP, START HIS OWN FAMILY AND ASBJORN WOULD BE LEFT ALL ALONE.

BUT NOT JUST YET.

THEY HAD A SIMILAR CONVERSATION EVERY TIME KOLL WENT OUT HUNTING.

BUT ASBJORN NEVER TIRED OF IT.

HE LIKED THE ROUTINE.

TIME TO WORK.

ASBJORN NEVER HAD TROUBLE WRITING.

TAK TAK TAK TAK TAK

HE COULD EASILY IMAGINE EVERY SCENE IN HIS STORIES.

TAK

TAK

PING

TAK TAK

BANG

BANG

TWO FAINT SHOTS AT 11 BROKE HIS CONCENTRATION.

TWO SHOTS MEANT KOLL HAD MISSED WITH THE FIRST SHOT. HE GRINNED KNOWING KOLL WOULD BE UPSET. HE'D TEASE HIM LATER.

IT WAS 1:30 WHEN HE NEXT LOOKED AT THE CLOCK.

KOLL SHOULD HAVE BEEN BACK A WHILE AGO...

ACK, HE WAS PROBABLY HAVING FUN. THE GARDEN COULD WAIT TILL TOMORROW.

TAK TAK TAK TAK TAK TAK TAK TA

BUT THE SEEDS OF DOUBT HAD STARTED IN ASHBJORN'S MIND.

HE FOUND IT HARDER TO FOCUS AND STRAINED TO HEAR ANY SIGN OF HIS SON.

HE STARTED GETTING UP TO LOOK OUT THE WINDOW AT EVERY IMAGINED SOUND.

BUT THERE WAS NO SIGN OF HIM.

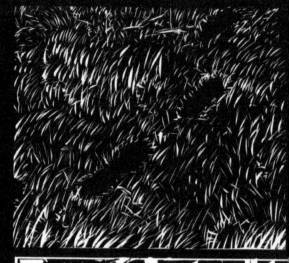

HE KEPT IMAGINING THAT KOLL WOULD APPEAR FROM BEHIND A TREE WITH A BIG BAG OF GAME AND A HUGE SMILE...

BUT NO.

NOTHING.

KOLL

HIS WORRY INCREASED.

WHY WAS THERE NO RESPONSE? WHAT COULD HAVE HAPPENED TO HIM?

OH GOD. THOSE GUNSHOTS! WHAT IF THERE HAD BEEN AN ACCIDENT? WHAT IF...

NO NO NO! STOP THINKING LIKE THAT.

DON'T PANIC.

IT WILL BE OK.

DON'T PANIC.

ANIMALS TAKE THE EASIEST ROUTE ACROSS A LANDSCAPE. AS THEY REPEAT THEIR JOURNEYS, NATURAL PATHS FORM.

WHILST SEARCHING FOR HIS SON, ASBJORN STARTED FOLLOWING ONE OF THESE PATHS WITHOUT REALISING IT.

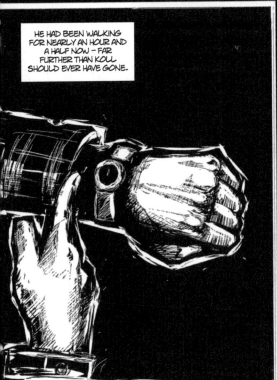

HE HAD BEEN WALKING FOR NEARLY AN HOUR AND A HALF NOW — FAR FURTHER THAN KOLL SHOULD EVER HAVE GONE.

BY NOW HIS VOICE WAS HOARSE AND HE COULDN'T SHOUT ANYMORE WITHOUT IT HURTING.

K-KOLL

KOLL

HE KNEW HIS VOICE WAS BECOMING QUIETER.

AND HE KNEW THAT WITH QUIETER SHOUTS THERE WAS LESS CHANCE THAT KOLL COULD HEAR HIM.

KOLL...?

IF, THAT WAS KOLL *STILL COULD* HEAR...

NO! HIS SON WAS ALIVE AND HE WOULD FIND HIM.

DESPITE THESE FORCED POSITIVE THOUGHTS, HE FELT A SUDDEN CHILL.

DEEP DOWN HE KNEW THAT HIS SON WAS DEAD. THE GRIEF THREATENED TO OVERWHELM HIM.

KOLL

BUT AS HE ENTERED A CLEARING AND SAW A DEAD TREE, HIS HEART *LEPT*.

KOLL WAS ALIVE!! BUT HE INSTANTLY SAW SHAME IN HIS SON'S FACE.

WHICH QUICKLY TURNED TO CONCERN WHEN KOLL SAW HIS FATHER'S FEATURES.

DAD ARE YOU OK?

WHERE HAVE YOU BEEN? WHAT HAPPENED??

I TRIED ALL DAY DAD, BUT I COULDN'T FIND ANY BIRDS.

I DIDN'T WANT TO COME HOME WITH NOTHING...I...I PROMISED YOU.....

I PROMISED

AND YOU NEVER BREAK PROMISES.

OH KOLL,

WHAT USE ARE BIRDS IF YOU AREN'T HOME SAFE? I WAS SO WORRIED. IF ANYTHING HAPPENED TO YOU I...

HE HELD HIM FOR A WHILE. ENJOYING THE RELIEF.

HIS BOY WAS SAFE.

KOLL...

ASBJORN KNEW THAT KOLL DIDN'T LIKE HOLDING HANDS, BUT ASBJORN DIDN'T CARE. HIS SON WAS ALIVE AND HE WAS HAPPY.

AND ALL THREE WALKED BACK HOME WITH ASBJORN CARRYING THE GUN IN ONE HAND AND TIGHTLY SQUEEZING KOLL IN THE OTHER.

ONLY...

ONLY THERE WAS
NO SHOTGUN.

THERE WAS NO
LUNDEHUND.

AND ASBJORN'S TIGHT SQUEEZE HELD NOTHING.

ASBJORN WALKED THE LONG JOURNEY BACK TO HIS CABIN IN A HALLUCINOGENIC DAZE.

IT WAS THE SAME WALK HE HAD DONE EVERYDAY FOR THE LAST SIX YEARS.

EVER SINCE KOLL HAD RUN AWAY AND SHOT HIMSELF.

ASBJORN AND HIS
SON HAD A ROUTINE...

A Lighter Note...

In the 3rd century BC, Ashoka abolished the slave trade and encouraged people to treat slaves well in the Maurya Empire, which covered the majority of India. He stopped short of abolishing slavery itself.

In 1963, the UAE abolished slavery and was one of the last countries to do so.

As of 2011, there are more human slaves alive than at any time in human history.

Writer/Creator
Neil Gibson

Illustrator
Heru Prasetyo Djalal

RAJEEV WAS BORN IN KERALA, SOUTH INDIA.

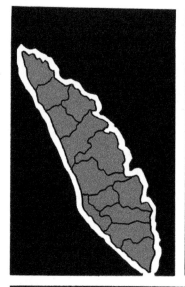

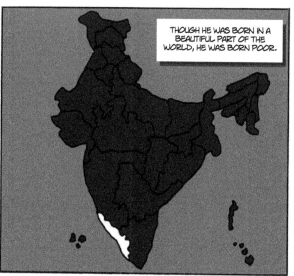

THOUGH HE WAS BORN IN A BEAUTIFUL PART OF THE WORLD, HE WAS BORN POOR.

THE SON OF A MENIAL LABOURER IN A VILLAGE WHICH ONLY SPOKE MALAYALUM.

HE GREW UP A GENTLE MORAL SOUL. THERE WAS LITTLE REMARKABLE ABOUT HIM.

HE ENJOYED CRICKET.

BUT WAS THOROUGHLY AVERAGE.

WHEN HE GREW UP, HE SOON DISCOVERED THAT JOB PROSPECTS IN KERALA WERE NOT GREAT.

NO MATTER HOW HARD YOU SEARCHED,

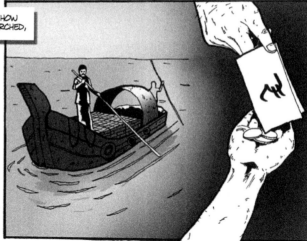

NO MATTER HOW HARD YOU WORKED,

THERE SIMPLY WEREN'T ENOUGH JOBS THAT REQUIRED FULL TIME WORKERS.

SAW THE RICH GET MARRIED AND HE TOO WANTED A BEAUTIFUL WIFE.

BUT WHAT MOTHER WOULD ARRANGE FOR THEIR DAUGHTER TO MARRY A MAN WITH NO PROSPECTS.

HOW COULD HE SUPPORT A FAMILY,

WHEN HE COULDN'T SUPPORT HIMSELF?

BUT THOUGH SADDENED, HE WASN'T BITTER. HE ACCEPTED HIS LOT IN LIFE. HE KNEW THAT EVERYONE HAD PROBLEMS AND YOU HAD TO MAKE THE BEST OF YOUR SITUATION.

YOU'LL BE GONE TWO YEARS AND WILL WORK AS A GENERAL LABOURER.

MY FEE?

I NEED TO GO GET IT.

I'LL BE HERE.

HE HAD TO BORROW MONEY FROM ALMOST EVERYONE HE KNEW IN ORDER TO PAY THE AGENCY FEE.

HE ENTERED SERIOUS DEBT, BUT KNEW HE WOULD MORE THAN PAY IT BACK WHEN HE RETURNED.

WITHOUT REALISING IT, HE HAD JUST EXPERIENCED THE FIRST OF MANY EXPLOITATIVE PRACTICES THAT HE WAS TO ENCOUNTER.

HERE.

AS HE TOUCHED DOWN HE PROMISED HIMSELF THAT NO MATTER HOW BAD THINGS GOT HE WOULD STICK THIS OUT AND MAKE THE BEST OF THE SITUATION.

THIS WAS HIS *CHANCE* TO GET A FAMILY AND MAYBE START A SMALL BUSINESS BACK HOME.

ON THE PLANE HE WAS A LITTLE NERVOUS, BUT MOSTLY EXCITED.

AS SOON AS THEY ARRIVED, THE TONE WAS SET.

PUSHED,

HURRY ALONG!

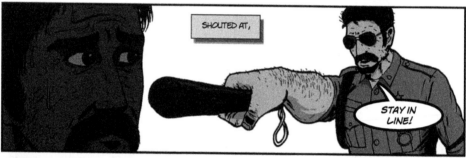

SHOUTED AT,

STAY IN LINE!

AND ROUNDED UP LIKE CATTLE,

NEW LINE. OVER THERE!

IT WAS A SCARY START FOR GENTLE RAJEEV.

IT WAS 47 DEGREES CELCIUS,

AND THEY WERE HERDED INTO A STINKING BUS WITH NO AIR-CONDITIONING AND DRIVEN TO THE LABOUR CAMP IN THE DESERT.

RAJEEV STARTED TO QUESTION HIS DECISION...

THEIR PASSPORTS WERE CONFISCATED, TRAPPING THEM.

AND THEY WERE NEVER PAID ON TIME.

OR IN FULL.

YET **ALL** OF THIS HE ENDURED WITHOUT COMPLAINT.

HE KNEW IT WASN'T FAIR.

ESPECIALLY AS HE SAW HOW OTHERS LIVED.

I'LL BUILD YOU FOUR MORE. YOU'LL MAKE MILLIONS.

BUT HE ENDURED AS WAS HIS GENTLE NATURE.

IT WAS WRONG, BUT IT WAS NOT AN INJUSTICE.

HE *HAD* KNOWINGLY SIGNED UP FOR THIS.

AND HE WAS GOING TO MAKE THE BEST OF IT.

ONE MORNING, THE WATER PUMP BROKE IN THE CAMP,

AND *NO ONE* CAME TO FIX IT.

AFTER THREE DAYS IN THE HEAT WITH NO SHOWER, NO CLEAN CLOTHES AND NOT EVEN BEING ABLE TO WASH HIS HANDS BEFORE EATING,

RAJEEV DECIDED THAT ENOUGH...

WAS *ENOUGH*.

WITH TWO OTHERS, RAJEEV LEFT CAMP WITHOUT PERMISSION AND COMPLAINED TO THE CAMP OWNER — A GUJARATI.

A DIFFERENT PROVINCE IN INDIA, BUT STILL A FELLOW COUNTRYMAN.

WE HAVE A COMPLAINT.

THE MAN'S NAME WAS CHANDRAN AND HE WAS AS HARD AS NAILS.

HE HAD A GOOD BUSINESS GOING WITH THESE LABOURERS.

...NO WATER FOR DAYS NOW...

HE LISTENED TO THEIR COMPLAINTS BUT HE WAS DAMNED IF HE WAS GOING TO LET THESE MALAYALUM SPOUTING CRETINS EAT INTO *HIS* PROFITS.

...DIRTY CONDITIONS AND ...

...ASKING FOR IS REASONABLE AND...

WHY SHOULD HE BUY A NEW PUMP TODAY WHEN HE COULD WAIT 2 MORE DAYS AND GET A SECOND HAND ONE HALF PRICE? IT WAS *SIMPLE* BUSINESS SENSE.

STOP!

THE WILL BE NO CHANGES.

BUT WE NEED WATER NOW.

OH BLOODY HELL..

A NEW PUMP WOULD COST HIM MORE THAN THESE THREE LOUTS WOULD EARN IN A YEAR.

HERE HE WAS GIVING THEM A JOB AND THEY HAD THE TEMERITY TO COMPLAIN TO HIM?

IT WOULD BE WRONG TO SAY SOMETHING SNAPPED INSIDE RAJEEV.

HE WAS STILL THE SAME GENTLE SOUL HE ALWAYS WAS.

ONLY NOW HE KNEW WHAT TO DO.

NOW HE WAS PART OF A CAUSE.

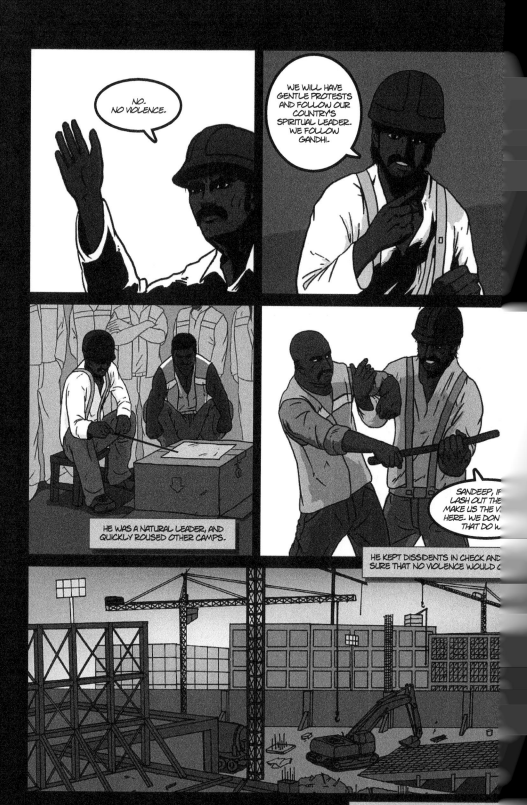

IN THE MIDDLE OF THE MORNING RUSH HOUR,

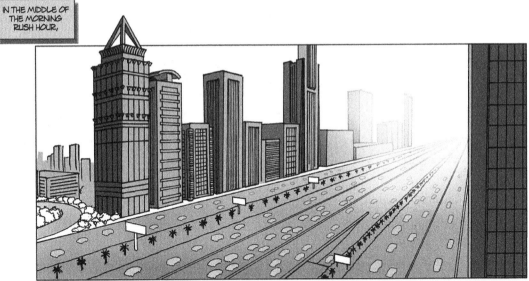

THEY WALKED OUT INTO SHEIK ZAYAD ROAD...

AND QUIETLY AND PEACEFULLY,

THEY GROUND THE CITY TO A HALT.

THOUSANDS OF COMMUTERS WERE JAMMED.

THEY SOON GOT FRUSTRATED.

AND ON LEAVING THEIR CARS,

THEY FOUND *PEACEFUL* PROTESTERS, SITTING ON CARDBOARD SO THEY WOULDN'T GET BURNT.

THE POLICE THOUGHT ABOUT USING VIOLENCE TO GET THEM TO MOVE.

BUT THE WITNESSES AND CAMERA PHONES DECIDED AGAINST THAT FOR THEM.

SO THEY JUST RADIOED IN THE PROBLEM,

AND PUSHED IT HIGHER UP FOR SOMEONE ELSE TO DEAL WITH.

AT THE SAME TIME, WORKERS CALMLY CAMPED OUT EN MASSE IN FRONT OF THE MAIN SHOPPING MALLS.

THEY SAT THERE IN EERIE SILENCE.

NO ONE FELT COMFORTABLE ENTERING.

THE SHOP OWNERS WERE NOT HAPPY.

THE AIRPORT WAS ALSO SHUT DOWN.

THE WORLD PRESS POUNCED ON THE
STORY WITH IMPRESSIVE SPEED.

AND EVERY TIME A JOURNALIST
ASKED "WHO ORGANISED THIS?"

THE ANSWER WAS THE SAME.

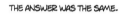

RAJEEV.

RAJEEV.

RAJEEV.

RAJEEV.

THEY QUICKLY FOUND HIM.

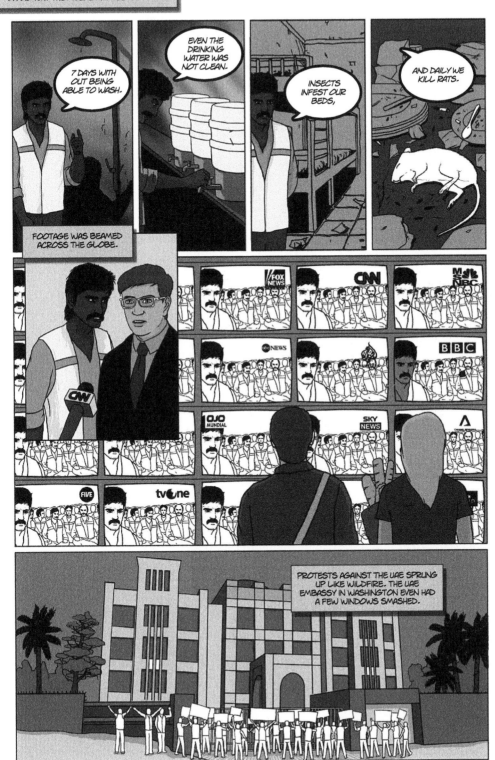

THROUGH A TRANSLATOR HE GENTLY AND HUMBLY SHOWED THE PRESS THE CONDITIONS THEY LIVED IN AND WHY THEY WERE PROTESTING.

7 DAYS WITH OUT BEING ABLE TO WASH.

EVEN THE DRINKING WATER WAS NOT CLEAN.

INSECTS INFEST OUR BEDS,

AND DAILY WE KILL RATS.

FOOTAGE WAS BEAMED ACROSS THE GLOBE.

PROTESTS AGAINST THE UAE SPRUNG UP LIKE WILDFIRE. THE UAE EMBASSY IN WASHINGTON EVEN HAD A FEW WINDOWS SMASHED.

59

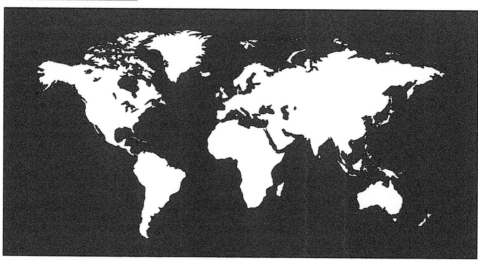

WORLD OPINION WAS HARSH.

THE DUBAI GOVERNMENT ISSUED A COMMAND AND THE LABOUR COMPANY WAS GIVEN STERN INSTRUCTIONS.

WITHIN AN INCREDIBLE 3 DAYS, RAJEEV'S MAIN CREW HAD A NEW CAMP ASSEMBLED OUT OF PORTACABINS. CHANDRAN LEFT THE COMPANY.

THEY NO LONGER HAD 8 PEOPLE TO A ROOM AND 32 TO A TOILET.

THEY EVEN HAD A MAKESHIFT CRICKET PITCH BUILT.

RAJEEV WAS HAPPY.

BUT HIS CO-WORKERS...

WELL....

THEY WERE *ECSTATIC.*

RAJEEV WAS PLEASED WITH WHAT HE HAD ACHIEVED.

SABOTAGING THE PUMP,

PAYING OFF SOME SUPPORTERS AND GUARDS,

AND ATTRACTING THE RATS.

HE HAD GOTTEN *LUCKY* WITH CHANDRAN'S ABRASIVE ATTITUDE,

AND *VERY* LUCKY WITH THE PRESS.

HE HAD ALWAYS BELIEVED THAT YOU SHOULD MAKE THE BEST OF YOUR SITUATION,

AND HE HAD PLAYED HIS HAND *PERFECTLY.*

THE CROWD HADN'T EVEN PUT HIM DOWN WHEN HE STARTED PLANNING WHAT HE WOULD DO NEXT WITH HIS *NEW POWER.*

END.

Windopayne...

"Rodrigo is one of the most eligible bachelors on the planet. Wealthy, generous, great to look at even with his scar and utterly mysterious."

- Plugin Magazine

Writer/Creator
Neil Gibson

Illustrator
Jan Wijngaard

PEOPLE NORMALLY REFER TO BLACK JANUARY AT THE START OF THE HORRORS, BUT THE SEEDS WERE PLANTED BEFORE THEN.

IT WAS 5 YEARS EARLIER WHEN WINDOPAYNES REALLY TOOK OFF.

RODRIGO PAYNE HAD TAKEN HIS FAMILY'S WEALTH AND BECAME ONE OF THE YOUNGEST BILLIONAIRES IN AMERICA WITH HIS BRILLIANT WINDOWPAYNE® INVENTION.

HE CONTROLLED THE COMPANY WITH RUTHLESS EFFICIENCY.

RODRIGO!

OVER HERE!

MR. PAYNE!

RODRIGO!

A QUOTE FOR OJO MUNDIAL?

THERE HE IS!

BUT HE NEVER TOOK WELL TO THE FAME.

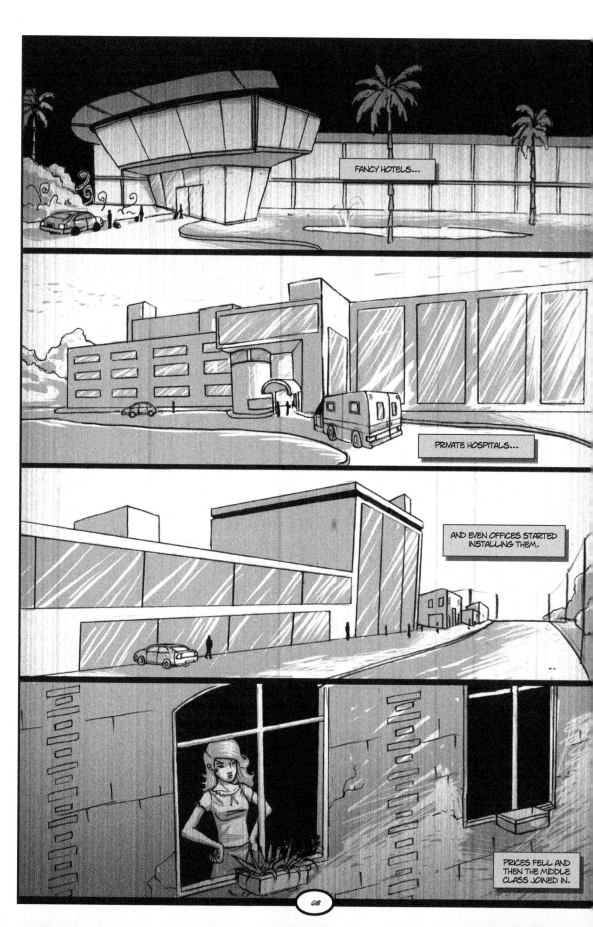

FANCY HOTELS...

PRIVATE HOSPITALS...

AND EVEN OFFICES STARTED INSTALLING THEM.

PRICES FELL AND THEN THE MIDDLE CLASS JOINED IN.

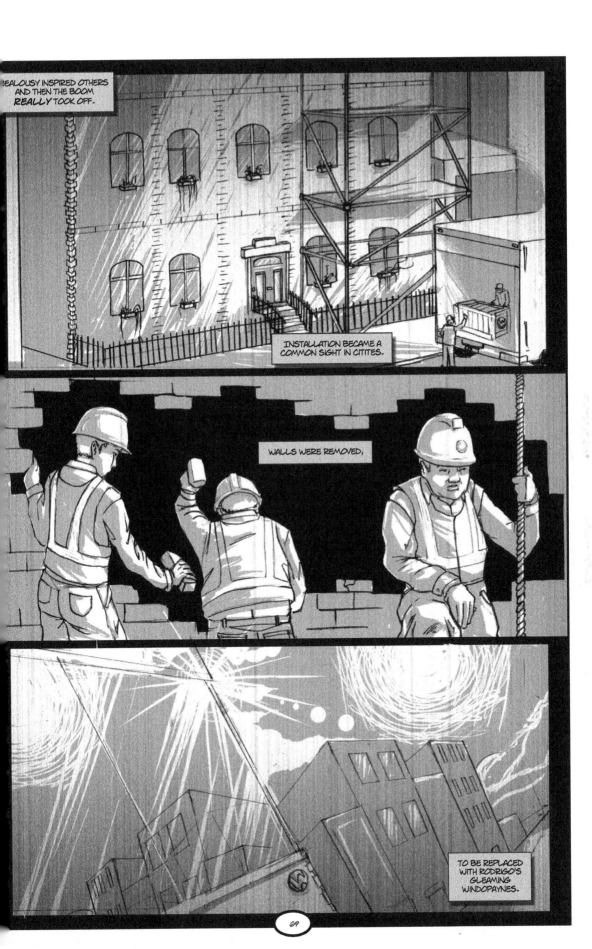

JEALOUSY INSPIRED OTHERS AND THEN THE BOOM REALLY TOOK OFF.

INSTALLATION BECAME A COMMON SIGHT IN CITITES.

WALLS WERE REMOVED,

TO BE REPLACED WITH RODRIGO'S GLEAMING WINDOPAYNES.

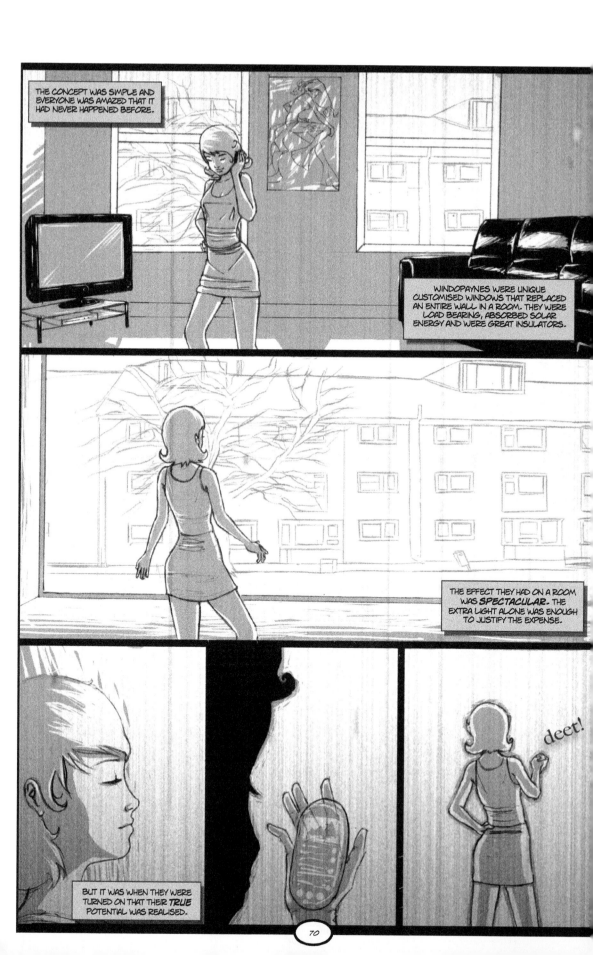

THE CONCEPT WAS SIMPLE AND EVERYONE WAS AMAZED THAT IT HAD NEVER HAPPENED BEFORE.

WINDOPAYNES WERE UNIQUE CUSTOMISED WINDOWS THAT REPLACED AN ENTIRE WALL IN A ROOM. THEY WERE LOAD BEARING, ABSORBED SOLAR ENERGY AND WERE GREAT INSULATORS.

THE EFFECT THEY HAD ON A ROOM WAS **SPECTACULAR**. THE EXTRA LIGHT ALONE WAS ENOUGH TO JUSTIFY THE EXPENSE.

BUT IT WAS WHEN THEY WERE TURNED ON THAT THEIR *TRUE* POTENTIAL WAS REALISED.

deet!

ANY IMAGE YOU LIKED COULD BE PORTRAYED ON THE WINDOW. IT COULD SHOW FAMILY PHOTOS, A TROPICAL RAINFOREST OR THE HONG KONG SKYLINE.

SOME PEOPLE USED IT FOR STILL IMAGES, BUT MOST PEOPLE USED THE VIDEO FUNCTION.

IF YOU WERE IN SEATTLE AND IT WAS DARK AND GREY OUTSIDE, YOU COULD CHANGE THE VIEW TO A LIVE FEED FROM BONDI BEACH.

PEOPLE CHOSE THEIR FAVOURITE VIEWS FROM THEIR WINDOWS.

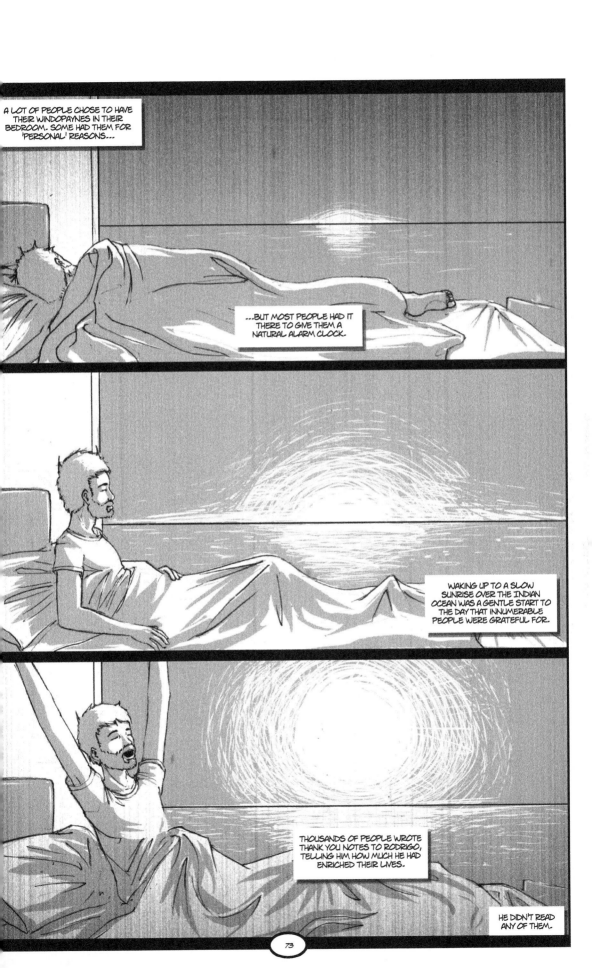

A LOT OF PEOPLE CHOSE TO HAVE THEIR WINDOPAYNES IN THEIR BEDROOM. SOME HAD THEM FOR 'PERSONAL' REASONS...

...BUT MOST PEOPLE HAD IT THERE TO GIVE THEM A NATURAL ALARM CLOCK.

WAKING UP TO A SLOW SUNRISE OVER THE INDIAN OCEAN WAS A GENTLE START TO THE DAY THAT INNUMERABLE PEOPLE WERE GRATEFUL FOR.

THOUSANDS OF PEOPLE WROTE THANK YOU NOTES TO RODRIGO, TELLING HIM HOW MUCH HE HAD ENRICHED THEIR LIVES.

HE DIDN'T READ ANY OF THEM.

HE WATCHED A
WALL OF FLAMES.

WHAT ONLY *HE* KNEW WAS THAT HE COULD PICK OUT ANY WINDOPAYNE ON THE PLANET...

England
Birmingham
Edgsbaston
Selly Oak
Dawlish Street
House 157

INITIATE

...AND SHORT OUT ITS COOLING SYSTEM.

WITHIN 50 MINUTES THE SELECTED WINDOWPAYNE WOULD BE RED HOT.

WITHIN AN HOUR, IT WOULD CONSUME ANY BUILDING IT WAS IN.

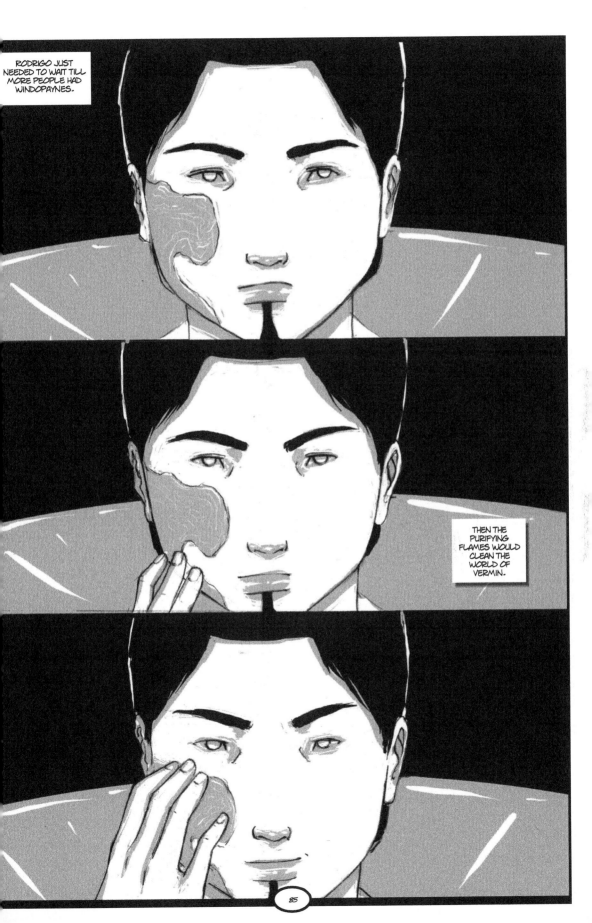

AND RODRIGO WOULD WATCH IT ALL ON HIS WINDOPAYNE.

The Game...

First Name:	Not given
Last Name:	Soames (Assumed)
Birthdate:	25th Dec 1955 (Not verified)
Sex:	Male

"Keep trying, hold on, and always, always, always believe in yourself because if you don't, then who will sweetie?"

Marilyn Monroe

Writer/Creator
Neil Gibson

Illustrator
Ant Mercer

A RESTICTED WING OF A POPULAR HOSPITAL

RIVERCREEK HOSPITAL

THE END OF MORNING ROUNDS

AND OUR FINAL PATIENT...

DR SMITH, WOULD YOU READ THE CHART PLEASE?

NO! NOT AGAIN!

LEAVE ME, LEAVE ME JUST LEAVE ME ALONE!

HUH.

DOCTORS DOCTORS DOCTORS ALWAYS MEDICATING ME...

COULD I PLEASE HAVE A MOMENT ALONE WITH MR. SOAMES?

THANK YOU.

AHH...

ACTING CAN BE SO DEMANDING DON'T YOU THINK?

SO IS VIEWERSHIP FALLING OR SOMETHING? THAT WHY THEY SEND IN A FRESH FACE? A GOOD LOOKING ALPHA MALE?

I DON'T UNDERS...I TRANSFERRED HERE FROM ST. MARY'S. IT'S MY FIRST DAY.

I SEE.

BORING COVER STORY BY THE WAY.

WELL, DO YOU HAVE ANY IDEA WHEN THE GAME WILL END?

GAME? WHAT GAME?

OH DON'T ACT WITH ME NOW. WE'RE ALONE – THERE'S NO NEED.

BESIDES, I GROW SICK OF ACTING.

DO YOU KNOW, I THINK I WAS A GENIUS WHEN I PICKED THIS AFFLICTION.

YOU CHOSE YOUR CONDITION? YOU CHOSE TO BE PARANOID?

I HAD TO. WE ALL DID WHEN THE GAME STARTED.

AH YES. THE GAME...

WHY DON'T YOU TELL ME ABOUT THE GAME?

REALLY? THAT'S HOW YOU WANT TO PLAY THIS? YOU WANT TO MAINTAIN THE PRETENCE?

HUMOUR ME — IT IS MY FIRST DAY AND ALL.

...

FINE. I SEE YOU WON'T BREAK CHARACTER. I OF ALL PEOPLE SHOULD RESPECT THAT.

WE WERE ALL GIVEN A CHOICE OF WHICH AFFLICTION WE HAD TO ACT OUT. AGORAPHOBIA, CLAUSTROPHOBIA, CATATONIC STATE...

WE ALL HAD TO ACT LIKE THAT FULL TIME. TO EVERYONE.

I RECKONED THAT IT WOULD BE DIFFICULT TO ACT OUT PHOBIAS THAT I DIDN'T HAVE, SO I PICKED ONE THAT I THOUGHT WOULD DEVELOP NATURALLY AS I PLAYED THE GAME.

CLEVER DON'T YOU THINK?

HOW SO?

ISN'T IT OBVIOUS? I HAVE TO FAKE MY BEHAVIOUR EVERYDAY TO EVERYONE.

I DON'T KNOW WHO THE RINGER COULD BE.

I DON'T KNOW FOR SURE WHICH OF THE OTHER PATIENTS ARE REAL PATIENTS AND WHICH ARE FELLOW COMPETITORS WHO ARE JUST ACTING LIKE ME.

THOUGH I HAVE CLOCKED A FEW FOR CERTAIN.

THE BAD PLAYERS LEFT EARLY. THEY GAVE UP AND WERE "CURED". THEY COULDN'T FAKE THEIR SYMPTOMS AND REVEALED THAT IS WAS ALL A GAME. I DIDN'T HAVE THAT PROBLEM.

YOU KEEP SAYING THINGS IN THE PAST TENSE. WE HAD TO DO THIS, I DIDN'T HAVE THAT. WHY? IT SUGGESTS YOU THINK YOU NO LONGER HAVE TO.

... WELL ...

AND ANOTHER THING, AREN'T YOU JUST FAILING THE GAME NOW BY TELLING ME THIS?

NO NO, YOU GUYS DON'T COUNT. YOU ARE LIKE THAT PRIVATE ROOM IN 'BIG BROTHER'.

I GET TO TALK TO YOU WHEN I'M ALONE AND I CAN BE MYSELF AGAIN. IT WAS ONE OF THE RULES WHEN I SIGNED THAT TV CONTRACT.

AND WHO DO YOU THINK MADE THOSE RULES?

I CAN PLAY LANGUAGE GAMES TOO. YOU SAID "WHO DO YOU *THINK*" RATHER THAN JUST "WHO".

THAT IMPLIES THAT EITHER YOU GENUINELY DON'T BELIEVE ME ABOUT THE GAME...

OR YOU WANT TO *SHOW* ME THAT YOU DON'T BELIEVE ME - SHOW ME THAT *YOU THINK* I'M CRAZY. TRY TO GET ME TO *DOUBT MYSELF*. THE FIRST IS IMPOSSIBLE BECAUSE YOU WORK HERE.

THEREFORE, YOU WANT ME TO THINK THAT THERE IS NO GAME. THIS IS NEW PRESSURE TO MAKE ME QUIT! THAT'S WHY THEY SENT IN A NEW DOCTOR. THE END MUST BE NEAR!

THIS IS NOT SOME... KIND OF REALITY SHOW. THIS IS REAL LIFE.

NUH-HUH DOCTOR. THE CAMERAS DON'T LIE.

"THERE ARE CAMERAS EVERYWHERE IN THIS PLACE."

THE SECURITY CAMERAS? BUT THOSE ARE STANDARD IN PSYCHIATRIC WARDS.

AND BESIDES, THERE ARE NO CAMERAS IN THE ROOMS.

NO VISIBLE ONES, BUT I'M SURE THERE ARE HIDDEN ONES.

YOU HAVE AN EXPLANATION FOR EVERYTHING. AND FRANKLY IT ALL IS LOGICAL.

BUT AS YOU ARE A LOGICAL FELLOW, TELL ME THIS. WHY WOULD PEOPLE *WANT* TO SEE PEOPLE DO THIS? IT WOULD GET BORING.

HOW COULD ANY TV SHOW BE POPULAR ENOUGH AFTER YEARS OF SEEING THE SAME STUFF?

WHAT ABOUT LAWSUITS. SOME PLAYERS MIGHT ACTUALLY GO CRAZY AND THEN WHEN THE SHOW WAS OVER THEY COULD SUE THE PRODUCTION COMPANY.

IT DOESN'T MAKE SENSE DOES IT?

YOU'VE ALREADY COMMITTED *SO MUCH* TO THIS. WHICH IS WHY YOU FIND IT HARDER TO 'GIVE UP'.

IF YOU FACE THE TRUTH, IF YOU *ADMIT* THAT THIS IS A FANTASY, IT WILL MEAN THAT YOU HAVE WASTED *YEARS* FROM YOUR LIFE. AND NOT EVEN A FUN FANTASY THAT YOU ENJOY.

YOU'RE NOT HAPPY

BUT YOU *CAN* BE HAPPY

YES YOU HAVE WASTED SOME OF YOUR LIFE, BUT YOU STILL HAVE THE CHANCE FOR THE REST OF YOUR LIFE. IF YOU KEEP UP THIS FANTASY WORLD YOU WILL BE UNHAPPY *FOREVER*.

NICE TRY "DOC".

I CAME REAL CLOSE THERE.

DAMMIT, THIS ISN'T A GAME! THERE IS *NO* GAME!

I'M NOT TRYING TO CONVINCE YOU FOR *MY* BENEFIT.

I'M TRYING TO CONVINCE YOU FOR YOUR *LIFE.*

ONCE I WIN THE GAME, I'LL HAVE THE BEST LIFE IMAGINABLE. TEN MILLION DOLLARS. I JUST NEED TO WAIT FOR THE OTHERS TO CRACK FIRST.

BUT YOU INSPIRED ME. I HAVE A THEORY NOW.

I RECKON THERE ARE ONLY A FEW COMPETITORS LEFT. MAYBE JUST 2 OF US AND NEITHER OF US IS GOING TO GIVE IN. THAT MAKES BORING TELEVISION. SO THAT IS WHY THEY SEND IN YOU - THE NEW SUPER DOCTOR TO SPICE THINGS UP.

I CAN HARDLY GIVE UP NOW WHEN I'M SO CLOSE TO THE END. CAN YOU IMAGINE HOW I WOULD FEEL COMING *SECOND?*

...HOW MUCH LONGER WILL YOU HOLD OUT? WHAT HAPPENS IF THE OTHER PLAYER ALSO DOESN'T GIVE IN? WHAT IF YOU ARE HERE FOR 5 MORE YEARS?

OH, HE WILL CRACK.

I NEARLY DID.

END.

Cocaína...

"I am in favour of legalising drugs. According to my values system, if people want to kill themselves, they have every right to do so. Most of the harm that comes from drugs is because they are illegal"

Milton Friedman

Writer/Creator
Neil Gibson

Layout Artist
Olga-Mila Gots

Illustrator
Caspar Wijngaard

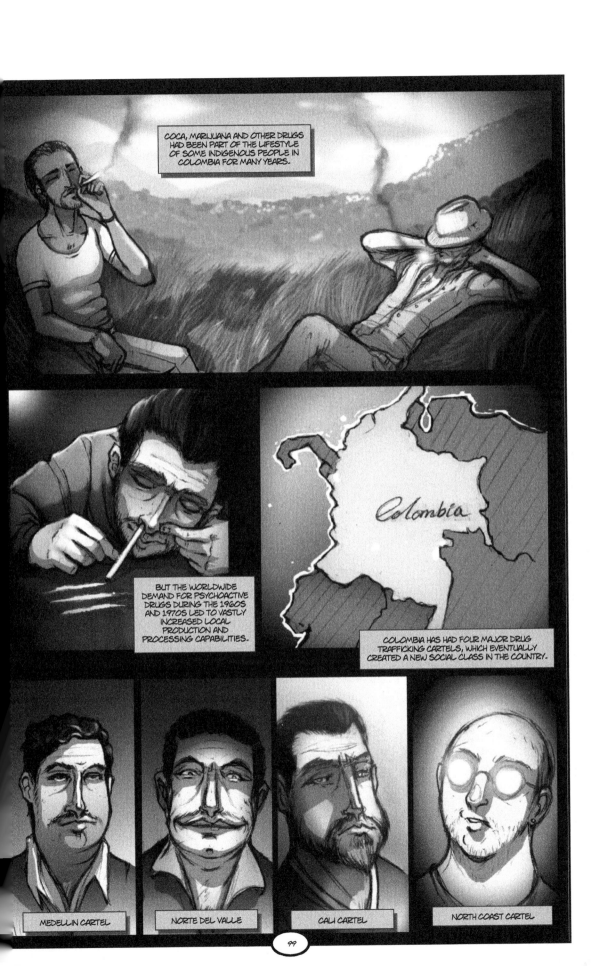

COCA, MARIJUANA AND OTHER DRUGS HAD BEEN PART OF THE LIFESTYLE OF SOME INDIGENOUS PEOPLE IN COLOMBIA FOR MANY YEARS.

BUT THE WORLDWIDE DEMAND FOR PSYCHOACTIVE DRUGS DURING THE 1960S AND 1970S LED TO VASTLY INCREASED LOCAL PRODUCTION AND PROCESSING CAPABILITIES.

Colombia

COLOMBIA HAS HAD FOUR MAJOR DRUG TRAFFICKING CARTELS, WHICH EVENTUALLY CREATED A NEW SOCIAL CLASS IN THE COUNTRY.

MEDELLIN CARTEL

NORTE DEL VALLE

CALI CARTEL

NORTH COAST CARTEL

AT ITS HEIGHT, THE MEDELLIN CARTEL ALONE WAS BRINGING IN $60 MILLION A DAY.

BUT THESE CARTELS WERE ALL DISBANDED.

IN ONE WAY...

... OR ANOTHER.

BUT DESPITE THE COLLAPSE OF THESE MAJOR CARTELS, COLOMBIA REMAINS THE LEADING PRODUCER OF COCA,

WITH APPROXIMATELY 70% OF THE TOTAL WORLD SHARE.

...D DOMINATES APPROXIMATELY ...0% OF THE COCAINE PROCESSING MARKET IN THE WORLD.

PROCESSING IS TYPICALLY LARGE SCALE.

BUT NOT ALWAYS.

PABLO WAS A DRUG PRODUCER AND DEALER, BUT NOT OUT OF CHOICE. IT WAS SIMPLY THE ONLY WAY HE COULD PROVIDE FOR HIS FAMILY.

HE TAUGHT HIS SON JUAN NOT TO DRINK,

NOT TO SMOKE,

NOT TO DISRESPECT WOMEN,

AND TO ALWAYS TRY TO GET PAID IN DOLLARS.

HE WANTED TO TEACH JUAN TO BE GOOD. HE WANTED A **BETTER LIFE** FOR HIS SON.

BUT IN THE END, HE TAUGHT HIM HOW TO SELL DRUGS.

TODAY YOUR CHILDHOOD ENDS.

FORGET WHAT I TAUGHT YOU BEFORE. WHEN YOU GROW UP YOU CAN CHOOSE TO DRINK IF

I HOPE TO GOD YOU DON'T BUT YOU CAN.

I DON'T EVEN MIND IF YOU SMOKE.

BUT NEVER, NEVER, NEVER, NEVER, **NEVER** SAMPLE THE PRODUCT.

THE PRODUCT IS POISON AND TAKING IT WILL RUIN YOU, OR WORSE, YOUR FAMILY.

IT WAS THE ONLY TIME HIS OTHERWISE JOLLY FATHER RAISED HIS VOICE AND THIS DEEPLY AFFECTED JUAN.

AND LIKE MOST PEOPLE HE ENJOYED DOING SOMETHING HE WAS GOOD AT.

BUT UNLIKE HIS FATHER, HE HAD *AMBITION.* HE SAW THE BIG PICTURE. IT HAD TAKEN HIS FATHER'S DEATH FOR HIM TO SEE CLEARLY.

ONCE HE REALISED THAT THE DRUGS WERE GOING TO BE HIS TRADE, HE STARTED PLANNING.

HE HIRED MEN TO DO THE RUNNING FOR HIM.

AND SO JUAN CONTINUED HIS ASCENT. HE GOT TO MEET THE HEAD OF A MINOR CARTEL — EL NUDILLO, THE KNUCKLE.

THIS WAY SIR.

AH! JUAN ISN'T IT?

GET SOME COFFEE FOR MR. JUAN WILL YOU? AND TELL ILLYANA WE ARE LEAVING SOON.

I HEAR GOOD THINGS ABOUT YOU.

THAT'S GOOD TO KNOW.

YOUR MEN NEVER DIP? THEY'RE ALL CLEAN?

I STRICTLY FORBID IT. I PAY THEM WELL AND NEVER HIRE DRUNKS OR ADDICTS.

AND YOU TRUST YOUR MEN WITH YOUR LIFE?

NO, BUT I TRUST THEM TO FOLLOW MY ORDERS.

GOOD.

MAYBE WE SHOULD TALK BUSINESS.

HOW FAMILIAR ARE YOU WITH THE DEA?

PAPI, I'M READY.

GO WAIT IN THE CAR.

THAT WAS THE FIRST TIME HE SAW ILLYANA.

AS I WAS SAYING, THE DEA...

EL NUDILLO TRIED HIM OUT ON A FEW SMUGGLING JOBS.

GOOD WORK. YOU'VE EARNED YOURSELF A BONUS.

IMPRESSED WITH THE RESULTS, EL NUDILLO HIRED JUAN TO WORK FOR HIM FULL TIME AND ABSORBED JUAN'S OPERATION INTO HIS OWN.

WHO'S THAT?

THE NEW BOSS. "HEAD OF QUALITY".

JUAN'S LIFE CHANGED SIGNIFICANTLY. THE MONEY, CARS AND GIRLS CAME SO EASILY NOW.

FROM MR. JUAN.

COME ON BABY, HAVE SOME WITH ME.

AS THE POWER INCREASED, SO DID THE *TEMPTATION* TO TRY THE DRUGS.

BUT HE REMEMBERED HIS FATHER BLEEDING IN THE STREET. HE KEPT HIS HEAD.

EVERY MONTH HE SENT HIS MOTHER MONEY, BUT HE STOPPED VISITING.

HE WAS *VERY BUSY* AFTER ALL, OR SO HE TOLD HIMSELF.

ERMM...

BOSS, YOU'RE UNDER MEDICATION. MAYBE YOU'RE NOT THINKING STRAIGHT RIGHT NOW, EH?

WHY NOT WAIT TILL MORNING BEFORE YOU DECIDE HUH?

THE BODYGUARD LOOKED AT PABLO IN THE SAME WAY A DOG LOOKS AT HIS MASTER.

EL NUDILLO SUDDENLY REALISED HOW MUCH DANGER HE WAS IN.

BLAM

...

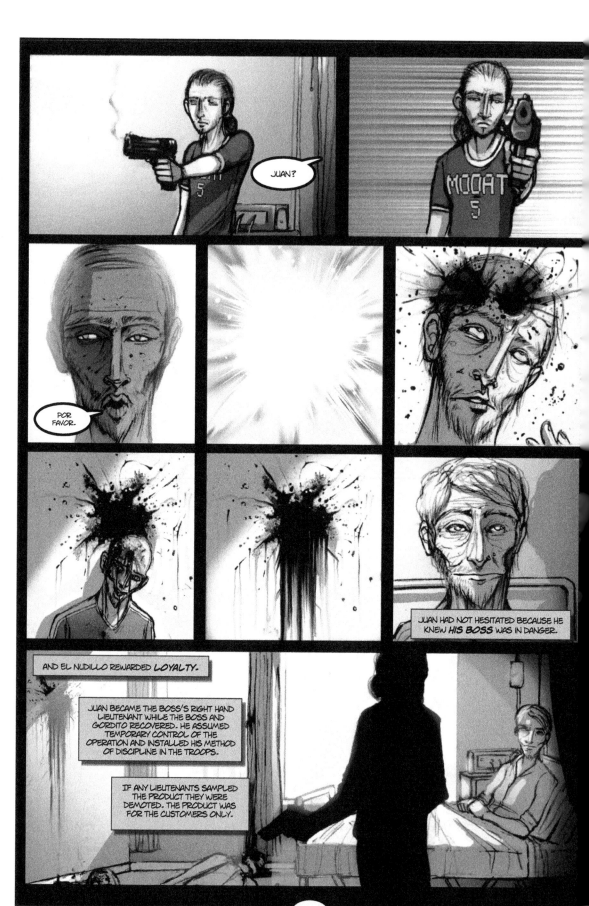

HE HAD A FEW TEETHING PROBLEMS ESTABLISHING HIS AUTHORITY.

WHY SHOULD I TAKE ORDERS FROM YOU?

BUT HE DELT WITH THEM.

WITH CLEANER SOBER MEN IN THE CRITICAL POSITIONS, PROFITS SLOWLY ROSE AND THE NUMBER OF BUSTS FELL.

índices de criminalidad

EL NUDILLO WAS STILL TOO ILL TO BE MOVED SO THE HOSPITAL ROOM WAS CONVERTED TO HIS COMMAND CENTRE. EVERYDAY JUAN BRIEFED HIS BOSS ON THE BUSINESS AND CHECKED IN ON GORDITO.

JUAN WAS INVITED TO EAT AT THE BOSS'S HOUSE WITH HIS WIFE AND DAUGHTER.

HE WAS RESPECTFUL THROUGHOUT AND WARY OF HIS POSITION,

BUT THE INEVITABLE HAPPENED.

HE WAS WORRIED ABOUT THIS TURN OF EVENTS.

BUT IT *COULD* WORK.

HE HAD **SAVED** THE BOSSES LIFE AND INCREASED HIS PROFITS. HE WAS LOYAL. HE NEVER TOUCHED THE PRODUCT.

HE WAS SMART ENOUGH NOT TO TRY AND FILL GORDITO'S SHOES. AND WISE ENOUGH TO ALWAYS CONSULT HIM, EVEN ON TRIVIAL MATTERS.

HE CONTINUED TO VISIT THE BOSS EVERYDAY IN HOSPITAL AND EVEN BROUGHT HOT MEXICAN TAMALES TO GORDITO WHEN HE WAS WELL ENOUGH TO EAT.

EL NUDILLO WAS A SMART MAN. RUTHLESS BUT LOGICAL. HE KNEW THAT JUAN WAS AN ASSET TO THE CARTEL.

YES. YES, THIS *COULD* WORK.

FAIRLY QUICKLY, JUAN AND ILLYANA DECIDED TO GET MARRIED.

I LOVE YOU.

IT OCCURRED TO ILLYANA THAT JUAN WAS ONLY DOING THIS TO CEMENT HIS POSITION IN THE CARTEL.

IT NEVER OCCURRED TO JUAN THAT HE WAS HER TICKET OUT OF OPPRESSION.

I LOVE YOU TOO.

ON THE DAY THEY CAME HOME FROM THE HOSPITAL ILLYANA NERVOUSLY ASKED HER FATHER FOR HIS BLESSING.

BUT SHE NEED NOT HAVE WORRIED – HE WAS *DELIGHTED* AND INSISTED THAT SHE INVITE JUAN TO THE HOUSE THE VERY NEXT DAY.

AS HE STARTED TO FEEL COLD, HE SAW ILLYANA'S FACE IN FRONT OF HIM.

THAT WAS THE LAST TIME HE SAW ILLYANA.

HEH!

HE WAS IN AGONY BUT LUCID, AND BIZARRELY HE SMILED.

HE RECOGNISED THAT DESPITE ALL HIS DISCIPLINE AND CARE, HE HAD BROKEN HIS FATHER'S GOLDEN RULE.

HE SHOULD NEVER HAVE SAMPLED THE PRODUCT.

END

Blame...

"It is not whether you win or lose,
it's how you place the blame"

Oscar Wilde

Writer/Creator
Neil Gibson

Illustrator
Atula Siriwardane

ARE YOU STILL DOWN HERE?

WHERE IS THAT PESKY NIGHT LIGHT?

TSK. IT'S SO DARK IN HERE THAT I CAN'T SEE WHAT NAUGHTY, SICK THINGS YOU MIGHT HAVE BEEN UP TO.

Click

AH, MUCH BETTER.

YOU KNOW, JOKES ASIDE, PEOPLE ACTUALLY DO PERFORM SICK ACTS ALL THE TIME....

CHILDREN PULL THE WINGS OFF OF HELPLESS INSECTS.

THEY BURN ANTS USING MAGNIFYING GLASSES.

I'VE SEEN THEM DO IT WITH *GLEE* ON THEIR FACES.

BUT I DON'T *BLAME* THEM.

SURE IT WAS SICK AND DISRESPECTFUL, BUT THEY HAD TO CUT UP HUMAN BEINGS.

NAZIS IN CONCENTRATION CAMPS USED TO SHOOT JEWS *FOR FUN.*

THEY HAD TO COPE SOMEHOW AND THEY BECAME NUMB TO THEIR SITUATION.

DOCTORS THERE EXPERIMENTED WITH IDENTICAL TWINS. THEY WOULD INFECT ONE WITH GANGRENE, AND LEAVE THE OTHER ONE HEALTHY.

THEY WOULD THEN KILL BOTH TWINS TO COMPARE THE BODIES IN A CLINICAL AUTOPSY.

BUT *AGAIN* I DON'T BLAME THEM.

THEY WERE PUT IN A POSITION OF POWER AND ABSOLUTE POWER CORRUPTS ABSOLUTELY.

I UNDERSTAND AND I FORGIVE THESE PEOPLE, AND MANY OTHERS...

MMMHH.

BUT YOU...

MHH

YOU TURNED A BLIND EYE WHILST DEAR FATHER RAPED ME...

AGAIN, AND AGAIN AND *AGAIN-*

AND THAT'S WHY...
...I'M GOING TO ENJOY THIS.
MMMHH! !
YOU MAY THINK THAT I'M CRAZY. THAT I'M SICK,
MMMHH!! MHH!!!

I DON'T BLAME YOU.

END.

WWW.NEILGIBSONCOMICS.COM

Definition of "Twisted":

Verb
Pronunciation: \ˈtwis-təd\

1. Unpleasantly or unhealthily abnormal
2. Forced out of the natural position by a twisting action

   Reference: The Compact Oxford English Dictionary ISBN 0-19-861186-2

Definition of "Dark":

Noun
Pronunciation: \ˈdärk\

1. The absence of light
2. A dark colour or shade

   Reference: The Compact Oxford English Dictionary ISBN 0-19-861186-2

Definition of "Twisted Dark":

Adjective (of sorts)
Pronunciation: \ˈtwis-təd ˈdärk\

1. A story with a sinister undertone, with characters that deviate from socially acceptable standards
2. An unusual smile that conveys several emotions, usually of a morbid nature

   Reference: The writer's own opinion

The Pushman...

Every day. Every *single* day.

Writer/Creator
Neil Gibson

Illustrator
Jan Wijngaard

YOSHI HIGUCHI IS A PUSHMAN ON THE TOKYO METRO SYSTEM.

WHEN THE TRAINS ARE CHOCKER-BLOCK FULL OF PASSENGERS,

HIS JOB IS TO PUSH MORE IN.

WHEN THE DOORS SHUT, HE REMAINS ON THE PLATFORM AND WATCHES THE TRAINS LEAVE.

AND WHEN EACH TRAIN LEAVES...

HE SEES THE SKYLINE FOR A MOMENT.

AND FOR A SHORT TIME, HE IS *HAPPY*.

THIS HADN'T BEEN HIS DREAM JOB AS A KID.

HE WANTED TO BE AN ARCHITECT.

HE SPENT HOURS AT SCHOOL JUST STARING AT BUILDINGS AND THINKING ABOUT THEIR DESIGN.

DESPITE HIS CLEAR PASSION AND TALENT, TOKYO UNIVERSITY HAD STRICT ENTRY REQUIREMENTS. YOU NEEDED GOOD GRADES TO BECOME A TODAII.

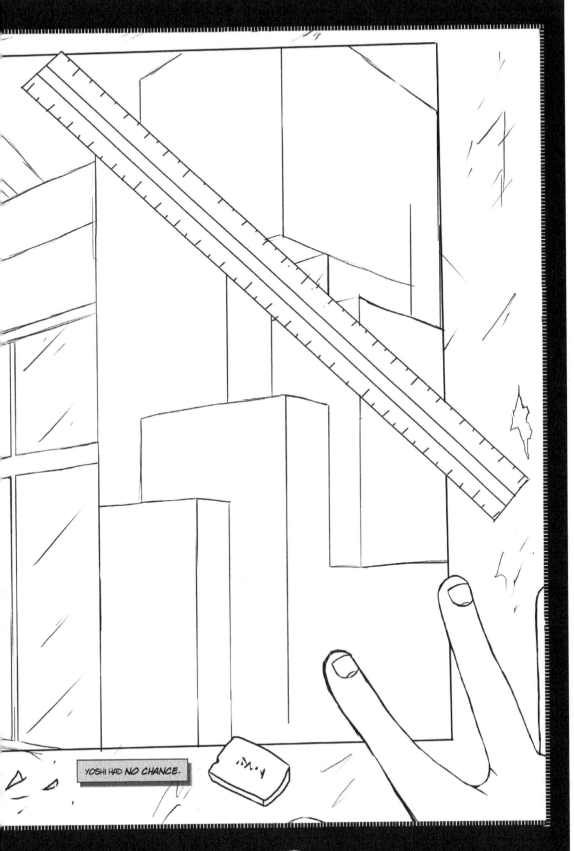

YOSHI HAD **NO CHANCE.**

HE HAD SO MANY SKETCHES WHICH HIS MOTHER WANTED TO THROW AWAY, SO WITH NOTHING TO LOSE HE POSTED THEM TO THE UNIVERSITY.

Væroy

BY SHEER LUCK, A GUEST LECTURER FROM NORWAY SAW HIS SAMPLES AND SAW HIMSELF IN THE YOUNG MAN.

Væroy

HE DECIDED TO GIVE YOSHI A CHANCE AND GRANTED HIM A PLACE.

YOU HAVE A LETTER.

IT WAS LIKE A DREAM COME TRUE FOR YOSHI.

YA SAH!

BUT DREAMS OFTEN FADE...

HIS FATHER GOT SICK AT THE START OF HIS FIRST TERM, CUTTING THE FAMILY INCOME.

YOSHI HAD NO CHOICE BUT TO DROP OUT AND FIND A JOB.

NOW EVERYDAY,

HE PUSHES PEOPLE.

PUSHING BECAME HIS LIFE.

HE NE[...] GO[...] PROMO[...]

HE DOESN'T KNOW IF HE WOULD EVER HAVE MADE IT AS AN ARCHITECT,

BUT HE RESENTS THE W[...] FOR TAKING AWAY HIS CH[...]

SOMETIMES THE PEOPLE
HE PUSHES REMIND HIM
OF SARDINES IN A TIN.

ALSO
SENTS HIS
RENTS.

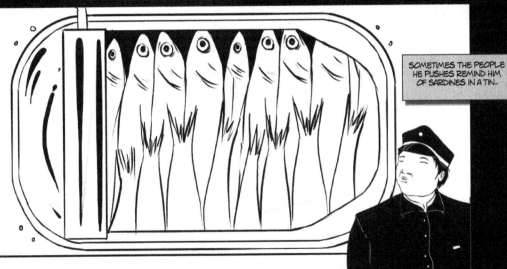

HIS FATHER IS STILL ILL AND
SOMETIMES YOSHI WISHES HE
WOULD JUST HURRY UP AND DIE.

HIS MOTHER IS *ALWAYS* ANGRY AND BOSSES HIM AROUND AT HOME.

SHE ROUTINELY WAKES HIM UP AT NIGHT AND SHOUTS AT HIM TO STOP SNORING.

PART OF HIM WONDERS WHETHER HE REALLY SNORES AT ALL OR IF HIS MOTHER JUST WANTS TO PUNISH SOMEONE FOR *HER* PREDICAMENT.

YET SIMPLE ROUTINE AND LAZINESS RESTRICT HIM FROM STANDING UP TO HER OR INDEED DOING SOMETHING ELSE WITH HIS LIFE.

SO EVERYDAY HE PUSHES PEOPLE AND EARNS HIS WAGE.

QUIETLY BOTTLING HIS ANGER AT THE LIFE HE THINKS HE HAS TO LEAD.

HE WATCHES THEM CRAMMING THEMSELVES INSIDE, BUT DESPITE HIS DISGUST HE SHOWS NO CONTEMPT.

IN A COUNTRY FAMED FOR CONCEALING TRUE FEELINGS, HE HAS BECOME AN EXPERT AT MASKING HIS EMOTIONS.

PUSHMEN DO THEIR JOBS STOICALLY AND PROFESSIONALLY. THEY KEEP THE TRAINS MOVING AND GET AS MANY PASSENGERS ON BOARD AS POSSIBLE.

YOSHI IS SLIGHTLY DIFFERENT FROM THE OTHERS THOUGH.

WHEN HE PUSHES PEOPLE, HE IS PUSHING AGAINST HIS LOST CAREER. HE PUSHES AGAINST ALL THOSE WOMEN WHO HAVE REJECTED HIM. HE PUSHES AGAINST ALL THE HARDSHIPS HE'S HAD TO ENDURE.

HE IS PUSHING BACK AGAINST *THE WORLD.*

HE REMAINS A PUSHMAN AND STANDS DUTIFULY STILL AS THE DOORS CLOSE.

AND WHEN EACH TRAIN LEAVES...

HE SEES THE SKYLINE.

AND FOR A SHORT TIME, HE IS HAPPY.

BECAUSE THE NEXT TRAIN WILL BE ALONG SOON.

EVERYDAY HE PUSHES PEOPLE...

AND HE *RELISHES* EACH ENCOUNTER.

END.

WWW.NEILGIBSONCOMICS.COM

A Heavenly Note...

"The world's Muslim population is expected to increase by about 35 percent in the next 20 years, rising from 1.6 billion in 2010 to 2.2 billion by 2030"

Pew Research Center's Forum on
Religion & Public Life

Writer/Creator
Neil Gibson

Illustrator
Heru Prasetyo Djalal

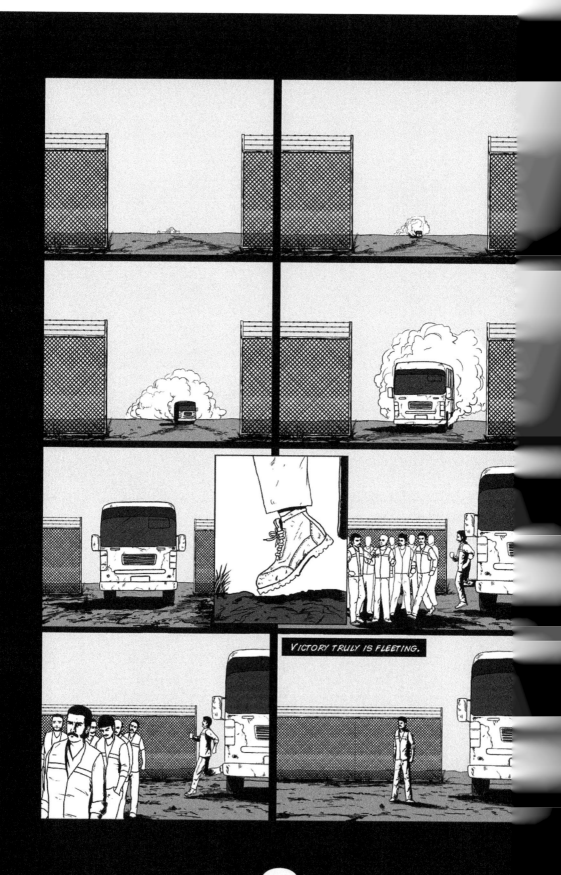

IT WAS A YEAR AFTER HE HAD ACHIEVED HIS SUCCESS AND CONDITIONS WERE CERTAINLY BETTER.

THEY HAD FOUR PEOPLE TO A ROOM NOW.

CLEAN DRINKING WATER, HOT SHOWERS.

PAYMENTS EVERY 2 MONTHS (ALBEIT WITH OCCASIONAL DELAYS).

EVEN A CRICKET PITCH WITH TENNIS BALL WRAPPED IN TAPE AS THE BALL..

BUT HE WAS NO LONGER THE HERO.

HE WAS NO LONGER SOMEBODY.

HE STILL GOT RESPECT, BUT NEW LABOURERS CAME IN WHO HAD NOT EXPERIENCED THE PRIOR CONDITIONS.

THEY DIDN'T KNOW WHO HE WAS AND WHAT HE HAD DONE FOR THEM.

HE HAD EXPERIENCED THE PLEASURE OF POWER.

BUT NOW HE HAD TO CONTEND WITH THE FACT THAT HE WAS STILL A LABOURER.

WORKING IN THE 50°C HEAT.

WITH NO PROSPECTS.

HE WONDERED HOW THIS COULD BE FAIR.

HOW COULD HE GO FROM BEING A HERO TO BEING A FORGOTTEN NOTHING?

OVER THE PAST 9 MONTHS THE GENTLE NATURE OF HIS HAD SLOWLY ERODED. BITTERNESS AND RESENTMENT HAD SLOWLY CONSUMED HIM.

HIS COWORKERS NOTICED HIS RESENTMENT AND ENCOURAGED HIM TO ATTEND A MOSQUE WITH THEM. ON A WHIM HE AGREED. MAYBE IT WOULD 'HELP HIM FIND PEACE'.

TO SAY HE DID NOT EXPECT MUCH, WOULD BE VERY POLITE.

BUT HE WAS WRONG.

THE BROTHERLY FEELING WAS PALPABLE.

THE PHYSICAL AND EMOTIONAL BOND FROM THEM ALL MOVING IN UNISON WAS CLEAR.

RAJEEV COULD FEEL SOMETHING UNEXPECTED STIRRING INSIDE OF HIM.

WHEN THE PRAYERS HAD FINISHED, A FEW STAYED FOR A TALK BY THE MULLAH.

AND THAT WAS WHEN HIS HEART STARTED TO POUND.

He listened to the Mullah preach and Rajeev felt hope for the first time in a long time.

The words spoke to him. He could see real meaning in them.

He looked around the room and quickly saw the true believers – they were the ones who were hanging on to every word the Mullah said.

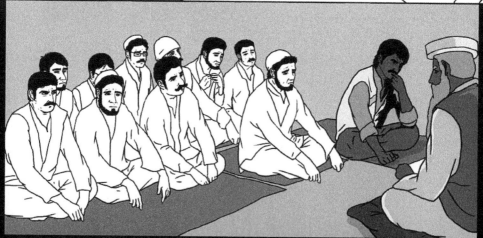

Rajeev listened intently too and knew immediately that he had found something great. He had never been a religious man.

He saw the light and converted to Islam. The speed at which it happened even shocked the mullah. But Rajeev was clear on what he wanted

HE STUDIED WITH FERVOUR AND STARTED TO LIVE HIS
LIFE AS THE PROPHET MOHAMMED WOULD HAVE DONE

HE ATTENDED THE DAILY PRAYERS AND STARTED DISCUSSING
THE SCHOLARS OF ISLAM....

ESPECIALLY WITH THE MULLAH

THE MULLAH EXPLAINED TO HIM HOW HE COULD TAKE HIS GOD GIVEN GIFT FOR COMMUNICATING HIS
ANGER AT INJUSTICE, AND USE IT TO CHANGE THE WORLD

HE REALISED HOW HE HAD BEEN MISGUIDED FOLLOWING GHANDI'S LEAD. HE SAW THAT HE HAD A
GIFT AND HE AGREED WITH THE MULLAH THAT HE COULD HELP CHANGE THE WORLD. HE HAD FOUND A
CAUSE

HE TURNED DOWN THE OFFERS HE HAD FOR MARRIAGE AND INSTEAD CHANNELED ALL HIS ENERGY INTO HIS NEW WORK WITH ALL THE ZEAL OF A CONVERT.

HE STARTED HOLDING TALKS IN THE CAMP AND AS BEFORE PEOPLE WOULD LISTEN.

HIS PASSION AND CLEAR BELIEF SHONE THROUGH AND WAS COMPELLING TO LISTEN TO.

HE STARTED TO CONVERT HIS FELLOW LABOURERS AND THE CAMP MOSQUE BECOME TOO SMALL.

HE WOULD PICK OUT THE TRUE BELIEVERS.

AND HELD PRIVATE TALKS WITH THE MULLAH TO FURTHER THEIR UNDERSTANDING OF ISLAM.

IT WAS A GLORIOUS DAY INDEED WHEN RAJEEV SAW HIS FIRST EXPLOSION IN THE ALMIGHTY'S NAME.
ALLAHUAKBAR!!
KABOOOM...!!

His young protege from Bengal had worn the suicide jacket with dignity and grace.

If he had fear in preparation, it was not shown.

BOOOM...!

The destruction was immense - gory and hideous.

It was wonderful....

HE DID NOT STAY LONG AT THE SCENE.
THE POLICE WOULD ARRIVE SOON

PEOPLE WERE ALREADY TAKING PHOTOS.
AND HE COULD NOT AFFORD TO BE SEEN.

HE HEADED TO THE RENDEVOUS WHERE THE
OTHERS WOULD PRAISE GOD FOR WHAT HAD
HAPPENED AND CELEBRATE THEIR CAUSE.

MORE PRAYER! HOW HE HATED IT.

FOOLS! KNEELING TO A GOD THAT DIDN'T EXIST.
PRAYING IN UNION LIKE FOOT SOLDIERS MARCHING.

THE KORAN, GOD AND ALL THE RELIGIOUS ARGUMENTS HE HAD MEMORISED – THEY WERE MERELY TOOLS.

RAJEEV COULD NOW COMMAND PEOPLE TO KILL THEMSELVES FOR THE CAUSE, AND THEY WOULD GLADLY DO IT.

RAJEEV NOW HAD REAL POWER, AND THAT WAS THE ONLY CAUSE THAT MATTERED.

Munchausen's Little Proxy...

"It's like I have a loaded gun in my mouth,
and I like the taste of metal."

Robert Downey Jr. on his addiction.

Writer/Creator
Neil Gibson

Illustrator
Caspar Wijngaard

CARNIVAL NIGHT IN THE SANTA TERESA SUBURB, RIO DE JANEIRO. A FANCY PARTY BY ALL MEASURES.

PEOPLE MADE AN EFFORT.

THEY WERE DRESSED TO IMPRESS.

BUT ULARA'S CHOICE...

WELL, IT BETRAYED HER *SECRET*.

OOKING BACK IT ALL SEEMS SO OBVIOUS, BUT AT THE TIME IT WAS ANYTHING BUT.

WHEN ULARA WAS 9, SHE STARTED TO GET SICK AND HAD TO STAY HOME FROM SCHOOL SOME DAYS. HER MOTHER WOULD TAKE CARE OF HER LITTLE ANGEL AND CALL THE DOCTOR.

AFTER A FEW DAYS SHE WOULD GET BETTER AND THAT WOULD BE THE END OF IT.

YET, A MONTH OR TWO WOULD PASS AND SHE WOULD GET SICK AGAIN.

I DON'T FEEL WELL.

AS SHE GOT OLDER, HER FATHER BECAME A LITTLE *SUSPICIOUS*, FEELING THAT HIS DAUGHTER TENDED TO EXAGGERATE HER CLAIMS.

PLEASE CALL JONATAS.

OF COURSE, DEAR.

BUT HE WOULD ACQUIESE TO HIS DOTING WIFE WHO FAWNED OVER THEIR DAUGHTER.

WHENEVER SHE GOT SICK, HE WOULD CALL THE FAMILY DOCTOR.

I DON'T KNOW WHAT TO TELL YOU.

BUT THE DOCTOR NEVER FOUND ANYTHING.

EVENTUALLY HER MOTHER ALSO BEGAN TO SUSPECT THAT ULARA WAS EITHER EXAGGERATING OR JUST FAKING. BUT SHE GOT SICK DURING THE HOLIDAYS TOO, AND ON DAYS WHEN THERE WAS A PARTY THAT SHE CLEARLY WANTED TO GO TO.

THE ONLY PATTERN THEY FOUND TO HER SICKNESS WAS THAT THE SYMPTOMS ALWAYS CHANGED, AND THEY GRADUALLY GOT WORSE – DIARRHOEA, VOMITING, STOMACH PAINS, CONVULSIONS...

DO YOU THINK THIS IS ALL CAUSED BY HER HEAD? DOES SHE DO THIS BECAUSE I SPEND TOO MUCH TIME AT THE OFFICE?

IS THIS ALL REALLY A PLOY FOR ATTENTION?

I DON'T KNOW.

IT'S POSSIBLE.

BUT DO YOU THINK WE SHOULD SEE A DIFFERENT DOCTOR? WHAT IF SHE REALLY IS SICK?

JONATAS HAS BEEN WITH US A LONG TIME, BUT HE'S NOT PERFECT.

I DON'T THINK I COULD FORGIVE MYSELF IF WE DIDN'T CHECK.

FINE, WE'LL GET ANOTHER DOCTOR.

A GOOD ONE. BUT HE CAN'T KNOW ANY OF HER HISTORY, OTHERWISE HE MIGHT BE BIASED AND THINK SHE IS FAKING.

FINE, WE'LL KEEP HIM IN THE DARK.

SO THEY CHANGED DOCTORS.

AND THE NEW DOCTOR FOUND SOMETHING.

SHE HAD BEEN OVERDOING ON IRON SUPPLEMENTS WITHOUT REALISING IT. SHE STOPPED TAKING THEM AND RAPIDLY RECOVERED.

MAURICIO'S REACTION WAS NOT HAPPINESS THAT SHE HAD GOTTEN BETTER...

WHAT HE FELT MOST WAS *RELIEF* THAT HIS DAUGHTER ACTUALLY *HAD* BEEN SICK THIS WHOLE TIME.

BUT THEN SHE STARTED GETTING SICK AGAIN...

MAURICIO DEVELOPED A TASTE FOR SCOTCH.

AS SHE GOT OLDER SHE BECAME MORE SOPHISTICATED IN HER CLAIMS.

SHE STARTED SEEING DIFFERENT DOCTORS ON HER OWN TO TRY AND 'CURE' HERSELF.

SHE PRODUCED SYMPTOMS THAT RESULTED IN LENGTHY AND COSTLY MEDICAL ANALYSIS, PROLONGED HOSPITAL STAY AND UNNECESSARY OPERATIONS.

WHENEVER SHE RETURNED FROM AN OPERATION SHE WAS HAPPY AGAIN.

EACH TIME MAURICIO AND HIS WIFE PRAYED THAT SHE WAS FINALLY CURED.

AND EACH TIME THEY *ALMOST* BELIEVED SHE WAS.

EVENTUALLY MAURICIO COULD STAND IT NO MORE AND THEY FOUND A SPECIALIST.

MR AND MRS DE SOUSA.

CAN I GET YOU ANY COFFEE?

NO THANK YOU, JUST TELL US WHAT YOU FOUND.

OK. ULARA REALLY IS SICK.

BUT IT IS A MENTAL DISORDER, NOT A PHYSICAL ONE.

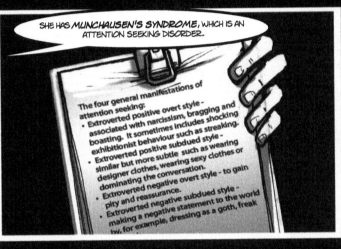

SHE HAS *MUNCHAUSEN'S SYNDROME*, WHICH IS AN ATTENTION SEEKING DISORDER.

The four general manifestations of attention seeking:
- Extroverted positive overt style - associated with narcissism, bragging and boasting. It sometimes includes shocking exhibitionist behaviour such as streaking.
- Extroverted positive subdued style - similar but more subtle such as wearing designer clothes, wearing sexy clothes or dominating the conversation.
- Extroverted negative overt style - to gain pity and reassurance.
- Extroverted negative subdued style - making a negative statement to the world by, for example, dressing as a goth, freak

ULARA'S REASON FOR DECEPTION IS NOT TO ESCAPE SOMETHING. INSTEAD, SHE SUFFERS FROM AN APPARENT DEEP-SEATED *NEED* TO BE SICK

A NEED WHICH CAN IMPEL HER TO INJURE OR POISON HERSELF IN AN EFFORT TO SUSTAIN THE ILLUSION OF ORGANIC ILLNESS.

SOMETIMES SHE GENUINELY *HAS* BEEN SICK, BUT I SUSPECT THAT SHE HAD MADE HERSELF BE SICK, FOR EXAMPLE BY DELIBERATELY INGESTING POISON.

FRANKLY IT SHOULD'VE BEEN DIAGNOSED LONG AGO.

MY BABY...

WHAT CAUSED THIS?

YOU THINK WE CAUSED THIS...

DIFFICULT TO SAY.

STATISTICS SUGGEST ABUSE OR NEGLECT AS A CHILD, OR A HISTORY OF FREQUENT ILLNESSES.

THIS... TRAVESTY!?!

I'M NOT SAYING THAT SIR, I'M JUST LISTING POSSIBLE CAUSES.

WHAT I DO KNOW IS THAT YOU WANT TO HELP YOUR DAUGHTER AND THAT IS WHAT WE SHOULD FOCUS ON.

...

LET'S DISCUSS TREATMENT OPTIONS...

THEY CHOSE THE GENTLE FACE SAVING OPTION. ULARA AGREED TO SEE A MENTAL HEALTH SPECIALIST TWICE A WEEK, RATHER THAN GO TO A PSYCHIATRIC WARD.

MAURICIO NEVER FORGAVE HIMSELF, OR HIS WIFE.

HE STARTED TAKING LONGER BUSINESS TRIPS.

ULARA ADJUSTED QUICKLY TO THE THERAPY AND STOPPED SEEING DOCTORS.

...AND THEN SHE HAD TO GO AND WEAR THE DRESS.

FOR YOUR NEW LIFE.

THANK YOU! YOU'LL COME VISIT ME IN AMERICA, RIGHT?

I'LL TAKE IT.

AGAINST THE ADVICE, SHE WANTED A FRESH START AND MAURICIO WAS HAPPY TO HELP.

SEEING HER REMINDED HIM THAT HE HAD FAILED HER, AND PART OF HIM WAS GLAD TO SEE HER GO.

SHE FOUND AN APARTMENT.

SHE FOUND A JOB.

FLUENT IN PORTUGESE AND SPANISH...

SHE FOUND SOME FRIENDS.

HI, I'M ULARA.

EVENTUALLY SHE ALSO FOUND LOVE.

ULARA AND NIGEL PAYNE GOT MARRIED IN THE SUMMER OF 1998. THEY SETTLED NEAR HIS FAMILY HOME.

A YEAR LATER A MIDWIFE DELIVERED THEIR BABY AT HOME.

WHAT A FINE LOOKING BOY.

WE WANT TO NAME HIM RODRIGO – AFTER GRANDPA.

THAT WOULD...THAT WOULD MAKE ME VERY HAPPY.

HE GREW UP A HEALTHY, HAPPY AND MUCH LOVED BOY.

HE WAS FOUR WHEN HE WAS ADMITTED TO THE HOSPITAL FOR THE FIRST TIME.

HE HAS A [L]UMP IN HIS THROAT.

THE TESTS SHOWED THAT IT WAS BENIGN, BUT THE DOCTORS DECIDED TO HAVE IT REMOVED.

DURING THE SURGERY, ULARA WAS BESIDE HERSELF WITH WORRY.

THE DOCTORS AND NURSES CONSOLED HER THROUGHOUT.

[H]E WENT HOME FIT AND HEALTHY. BUT A FEW WEEKS LATER ULARA NOTICED A CLEAR LIQUID DISCHARGE ON HIS LEFT EAR.

GOOD MORNING! [W]HAT'S THIS ON YOUR EAR?

MAMA?

AFTER TWO DAYS, ULARA TOOK HIM BACK TO THE HOSPITAL.

WE DON'T KNOW WHAT IT IS YET. WHILE WE RUN MORE TESTS WE THINK HE SHOULD STAY WITH US.

IF YOU THINK IT'S BEST...

IT WAS ODOURLESS AND OCCASIONALLY CONTAINED BUBBLES. BUT IT STOPPED APPEARING SOON AFTER ADMISSION.

WE'LL KEEP TESTING. BUT AT LEAST THE DISCHARGE HAS STOPPED.

PLEASE... KEEP HIM HERE UNTIL YOU'RE SURE HE IS SAFE.

COMPUTERISED TOMOGRAMS OF THE TEMPORAL BONES WERE NORMAL. IT MADE NO SENSE.

THERE ARE NO SYMPTOMS, SIR.

YOU CAN'T SAY THAT! THOSE TESTUBES ARE PROOF!

WHEN RODRIGO HAD BEEN SICK, SHE HAD ALL THOSE DOCTORS PAYING HER ATTENTION.

GOD, IT FELT GOOD.

SO SHE HAD PROLONGED THE FEELING. JUST FOR A BIT.

SHE LEFT SALIVA ON HIS EAR WHICH HAD TRICKED THE DOCTORS.

BUT NOW HER FATHER WAS SUSPICIOUS. IT WAS GETTING DANGEROUS.

BUT SHE HAD TASTED HER OLD ADDICTION AND SHE COULDN'T FIGHT IT. SHE STARTED PLANNING.

SHE BOUGHT RODRIGO SOME MARBLES AND LEFT THEM OUT WHERE HE PLAYED.

EVENTUALLY HE TRIPPED...

AHH!

SO AS AN UNSATISISFIED ADDICT...

BUT ALL HE NEEDED WAS A PLASTER.

SHE ESCALATED.

MAURICIO FLEW OVER AS SOON AS HE HEARD ABOUT HIS GRANDSON.

ULARA! LET ME IN. WE NEED TO RESOLVE THIS.

ULARA REFUSED TO MEET HIM.

SO HE ARRANGED A PRIVATE CHAT WITH NIGEL.

IT DID NOT GO WELL.

MAURICIO RETURNED TO BRAZIL WITHOUT SEEING RODRIGO, BUT WITH A CLEAR CONSCIENCE. HE BOUGHT THE BEST WHISKY ON SALE AT DUTY FREE.

MMYAAGHH!!

FUD

DMFFFE

GRRHHHAAA

PART OF ULARA FELT RELIEF AT THE BEATING. SHE FELT SHE DESERVED IT FOR WHAT SHE HAD DONE.

MOST OF HER JUST FELT PAIN.

MY GOD! WE GOTTA STOP THAT.

POLICE! FREEZE!

MY SON? IS HE OK?

THE PARAMEDICS HAVE HIM. THEY ALSO HAVE YOUR WIFE YOU SICKO.

The Last Laugh...

Writer/Creator
Neil Gibson

Illustrator
Dan West

THERE ARE OVER 10,000 SPECIES OF ANTS.

MOST ANTS ARE SCAVENGERS, AS EVERY PICNIC ENTHUSIAST KNOWS.

ONCE THEY FIND A FOOD SOURCE THEY WILL DO THEIR BEST TO TRANSPORT IT BACK TO THEIR COLONY.

OTHER ANTS LIKE THE SIAFU ARE PREDATORY. THEY KILL FOR FOOD.

THE SIAFU ARE AFRICA'S TOP PREDATOR. THEY KILL MORE PREY THAN ANY OTHER SPECIES.

HOWEVER, THERE ARE MORE THAN 200 SPECIES THAT ARE FARMERS.

THEY FARM FUNGI.

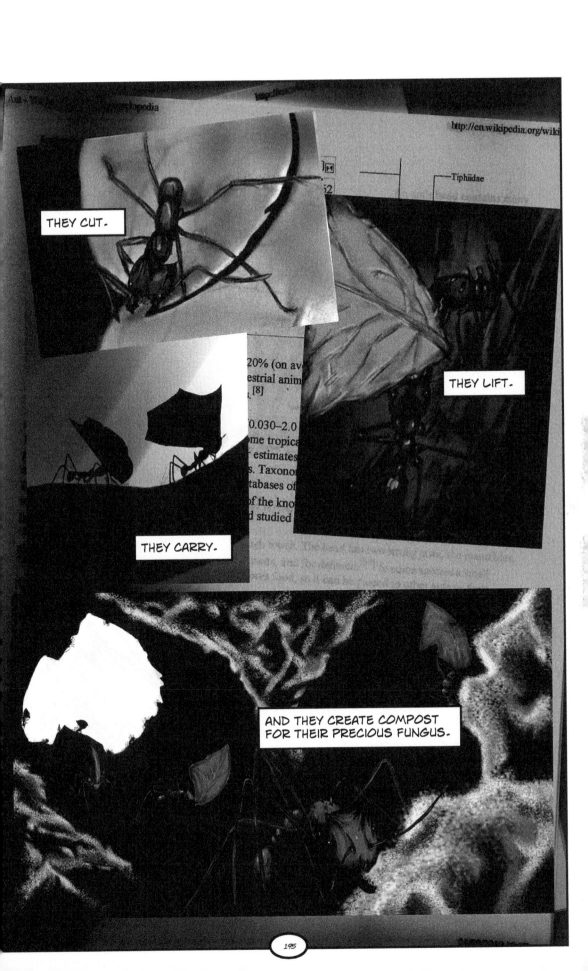

THEY CUT.

THEY LIFT.

THEY CARRY.

AND THEY CREATE COMPOST
FOR THEIR PRECIOUS FUNGUS.

THEY LOOK AFTER THEIR CROP WITH CARE.

FERTILISING IT.

PRUNING IT.

THEY EVEN FUMIGATE IT TO KEEP IT PARASITE-FREE.

...terranean ...cies are completely blind. Some ants such as Australia's bulldog ant, however, have exceptional vision. Two antennae ("feelers") are attached to the head... organs d...

THE ANTS HAVE COMPLETE CONTROL OF THEIR FARM.

...abdomen") of the reproductive, respiratory (tracheae) and egg-laying structures modified into sting...

Polymorphism

BUT A PHILOSOPHER MIGHT ASK WHO THE REAL FARMER IS...

SOME FUNGI HAVE DEVELOPED SPECIALISED SPORES.

THESE SPORES GET INSIDE SOME OF THE ANTS BODY AND RELEASE A PHEROMONE THAT SCRAMBLES THEIR BRAINS.

DISORIENTATED AND CONFUSED...

THE ANTS CLIMB AS HIGH AS THEY CAN AND CLAMP THEMSELVES THERE WITH THEIR JAWS.

THE FUNGUS FRUITS IN THE ANT

EVENTUALLY ERUPTING FROM THE ANT'S BRAIN

AND SPRINKLES NEW SPORES ON THE UNSUSPECTING ANTS BELOW.

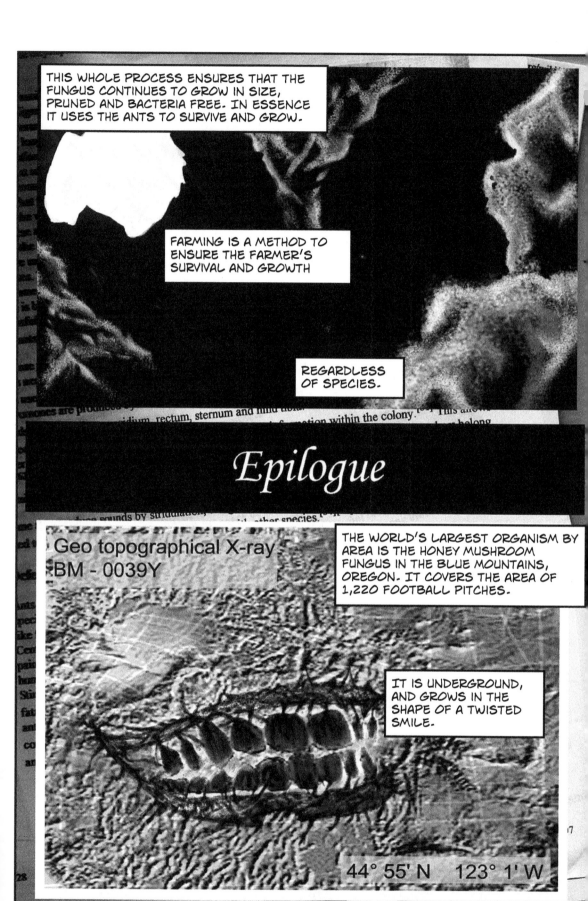

THIS WHOLE PROCESS ENSURES THAT THE FUNGUS CONTINUES TO GROW IN SIZE, PRUNED AND BACTERIA FREE. IN ESSENCE IT USES THE ANTS TO SURVIVE AND GROW.

FARMING IS A METHOD TO ENSURE THE FARMER'S SURVIVAL AND GROWTH

REGARDLESS OF SPECIES.

Epilogue

Geo topographical X-ray
BM - 0039Y

THE WORLD'S LARGEST ORGANISM BY AREA IS THE HONEY MUSHROOM FUNGUS IN THE BLUE MOUNTAINS, OREGON. IT COVERS THE AREA OF 1,220 FOOTBALL PITCHES.

IT IS UNDERGROUND, AND GROWS IN THE SHAPE OF A TWISTED SMILE.

44° 55' N   123° 1' W

A note from Neil...

Thank you for reading my first collection. If you enjoyed it, please join our Twisted Dark facebook page where you will get updates, discounts, and free stories (some in colour). Joining our facebook page will also make you thinner, sexier and taller. Fact.

Check out our other volumes. See how **all** the stories slowly start to connect with each other. Available from selected comic shops and from our website at www.neilgibsoncomics.com .